For Andrea (the joyful) Tickle
1986 - 2012

Miss ya

The Persian Alphabet

We want to simplify your Persian learning journey as it is such a unique & enigmatic language. There are 32 official Persian letters. The letters change form depending on their position in a word or when they appear separate from other letters. For example, the letter g͟hayn غ has four ways of being written depending on where it appears in any given word:

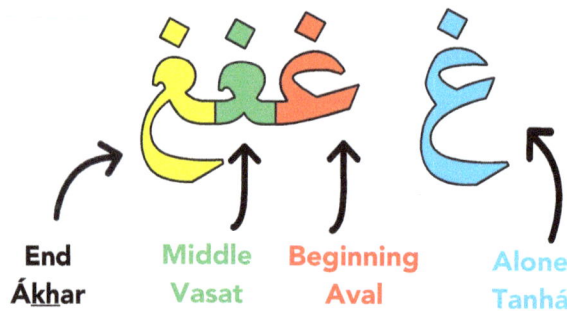

End
Á͟khar

Middle
Vasat

Beginning
Aval

Alone
Tanhá

It is important to note that Persian books are read from right to left (←). There are 7 separate/stand-alone letters that do not connect in the same way to adjacent letters (these will be depicted in blue). They are:

Stand alone
Tanhá vámístan

The short vowels a, e & o are usually omitted in literature and are depicted by markings above & below letters (ـــــ). They are not allocated a letter name, unlike their long vowel counterparts á: alef, í: ye & ú: váv (و ى آ).

Englisi	Farsi
A a	اَ ـَ
Á á	آ ا ا — 'alef
B b	ب ـبـ ـب — Be
D d	د ـد — dál
E e	اِ ـِ ـِ
F f	ف ـفـ ـف — fe
G g	گ ـگـ ـگ گ — gáf
H h	ه ـهـ ـه — he
H h	ح ـحـ ـح — he
Í í	ی ـیـ ـیـ — ye
J j	ج ـجـ ـج — jim
K k	ک ـکـ ـک ک — káf
L l	ل ـلـ ـل — lám

Englisi	Farsi
M m	م ـمـ ـم — mím
N n	ن ـنـ ـن — nún
O o	اُ ـُ
P p	پ ـپـ ـپ — pe
Q q	ق ـقـ ـق — qáf
R r	ر ـر — re
S s	س ـسـ ـس — sin
S s	ص ـصـ ـص — sád
S s	ث ـثـ ـث — se
T t	ت ـتـ ـت — te
T t	ط ـطـ ـط — tá
Ú ú	و ـو — váv
V v	و ـو — váv

Englisi	Farsi
Y y	ی ـیـ ـیـ — ye
Z z	ذ ـذ — zál
Z z	ز ـز — ze
Z z	ض ـضـ ـض — zád
Z z	ظ ـظـ ـظ — zá
Ch ch	چ ـچـ ـچ — che
Gh gh	غ ـغـ ـغ — ghayn
Kh kh	خ ـخـ ـخ — khe
Sh sh	ش ـشـ ـش — shín
Zh zh	ژ ـژ — zhe
'	ع ـعـ ـع — ayn

Letter Guide©

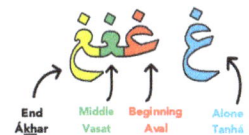

غ ـغـ غ غ

End Ákhar → | Middle Vasat ↑ | Beginning Aval ↑ | Alone Tanhá ↑

Pronunciation Guide©

Persian	English	Pronunciation
اَ	a	**a**nt
آ	á	**a**rm
ب	b	**b**at
د	d	**d**og
اِ	e	**e**nd
ف	f	**f**un
گ	g	**g**o
ه	h	**h**at
ح	h	**h**at
ی	í	m**ee**t
ج	j	**j**et
ک	k	**k**ey
ل	l	**l**ove
م	m	**m**e
ن	n	**n**ap
اُ	o	**o**n
پ	p	**p**at
ق	q/gh*	me**r**ci
ر	r	**r**un
س	s	**s**un
ص	s	**s**un
ث	s	**s**un

Persian	English	Pronunciation
ت	t	**t**op
ط	t	**t**op
و	ú	m**oo**n
و	v	**v**an
ی	y	**y**es
ذ	z	**z**oo
ز	z	**z**oo
ض	z	**z**oo
ظ	z	**z**oo
چ	ch	**ch**air
غ	gh*	me**r**ci
خ	kh*	ba**ch**
ش	sh	**sh**are
ژ	zh	plea**s**ure
ع	'	uh-oh†

People with disability
Áfráde dáráye natavání
افراد دارای ناتَوانی

Background & guide for terminology used in our resources.

"People with disability often have a
preference for one term or the other.
If you are not sure,
It's okay to ask.

Person-first language (people with disability) should be used
when speaking to or about people with disability and
identity-first language (disabled people) are both used".

People with Disability Australia 2021

A person who has a visual disability

Fardí keh nábínáyí dárad

فَردی کِه نابینایی دارَد

í: as (ee) in m<u>ee</u>t
á: as (a) in <u>a</u>rm

A person who wears glasses

Fardí keh e'ynak estefádeh míkonad

فَردی کِه از عینَک اِستِفادِه می کُنَد

í: as (ee) in m<u>ee</u>t
á: as (a) in <u>a</u>rm

A person with a hearing disability

Fardí keh náshenéváyí dárad

فَردی کِه ناشِنِوایی دارَد

á: as (a) in arm
í: as (ee) in meet

A person who uses hearing aids

Fardí keh sama'k estefádeh míkonad

فَردی کِه از سَمَعک اِسِتفادِه می کنَد

í: as (ee) in m<u>ee</u>t
á: as (a) in <u>a</u>rm

A person with a physical disability

Fardí keh nátavání jesmí dárad

فَردی کِه ناتَوانی جِسمی دارَد

í: as (ee) in m<u>ee</u>t
á: as (a) in <u>a</u>rm

A person who uses a wheelchair

Fardí keh sandalíye <u>ch</u>ar<u>kh</u> dár estefádeh míkonad

فَردی کِه صَندَلیِ چَرخ دار اِستِفادِه میکُنَد

í: as (ee) in m<u>ee</u>t
á: as (a) in <u>a</u>rm

A person who has a cognitive/intellectual disability

Fardí keh nátavaníe zehní / shenákhtí dárad

فَردی کِه ناتَوانی ذِهنی / شِناختی دارَد

í: as (ee) in m<u>ee</u>t

á: as (a) in <u>a</u>rm

A person with epilepsy

Fardí mobtalá beh sar'

فَرد مُبتلا بِه صَرع

í: as (ee) in m<u>ee</u>t
á: as (a) in <u>a</u>rm

A person with autism
(on the autism spectrum)

Fard mobtalá beh útísm

فَرد مُبتلا بِه اوتیسم

á: as (a) in a<u>r</u>m

ú: as (oo) in m<u>oo</u>n

í: as (ee) in m<u>ee</u>t

A person with attention deficit disorder

Farde mobtalá beh ekhtelále kambúde tavajoh

فَردِ مُبتَلا بِه اِختِلالِ کَمبودِ تَوَجُّه

á: as (a) in <u>a</u>rm
ú: as (oo) in m<u>oo</u>n

A person with one arm

Fardí bá yek bázú

فَردی با یِک بازو

í: as (ee) in m<u>ee</u>t
á: as (a) in <u>a</u>rm
ú: as (oo) in m<u>oo</u>n

A person with one leg

Fardí bá yek pá

فَردی با یِک پا

í: as (ee) in m<u>ee</u>t
á: as (a) in <u>a</u>rm

A person with an acquired brain injury

Fardí bá ásíbe maghzí aktesábí

فَردی با آسیبِ مَغزی اکتِسابی

á: as (a) in arm
í: as (ee) in meet

A person with dementia

Fard mobtalá beh yád farámúshí

فَرد مُبتلا بِه یاد فَراموشی

á: as (a) in <u>a</u>rm
ú: as (oo) in m<u>oo</u>n
í: as (ee) in m<u>ee</u>t

A person with paraplegia

Fard mobtalá beh pár áple<u>zh</u>í

فَرد مُبتلا بِه پاراپلِژی

á: as (a) in <u>a</u>rm
í: as (ee) in m<u>ee</u>t

A person with quadriplegia

Fard mobtalá beh falaje <u>ch</u>ahár andám

فرد مُبتلا به فَلَجِ چَهار اندام

á: as (a) in <u>a</u>rm
í: as (ee) in m<u>ee</u>t

A person with depression

Farde mobtalá beh afsordegí

فَردِ مُبتلا بِه افسُردِگی

á: as (a) in <u>a</u>rm
í: as (ee) in m<u>ee</u>t

A person with anxiety

Farde mobtalá beh aztaráb

فَردِ مُبتلا بِه اضطَراب

á: as (a) in <u>a</u>rm

A person with diabetes

Fard mobtalá beh díábet

فَرد مُبتلا بِه دِيابِت

[maríze ghand]

í: as (ee) in m<u>ee</u>t
á: as (a) in <u>ar</u>m

A person with high blood pressure

Farde mabtalá beh feshár khúne bálá

فَردِ مُبتلا بِه فِشار خونِ بالا

á: as (a) in a̲rm
ú: as (oo) in mo̲o̲n

Quick Reference: Helpful Medical Words

English	Finglisi™	Persian
Glasses	e'ynak	عینَک
Hearing aid	sama'k	سَمَعک
Stethoscope	gúshí pezeshkí	گوشی پِزشکی
Blood Pressure	feshár khún	فِشار خون
Diabetes	díábet	دیابِت
Disability	nátavání	ناتَوانی
Brain	maghz	مَغز
Heart	ghalb	قَلب
Lung	ríeh	ریِه
Skin	púst	پوست
Bone	ostekhún	اُستِخوان
Kidney	kolíeh	کُلیِه
Eye	cheshm	چِشم
Ear	gúsh	گوش
Mouth	dahan	دَهان
English	Englísí	اِنگلیسی
Persian	Fársí	فارس

www.ingramcontent.com/pod-product-compliance
Lightning Source LLC
Chambersburg PA
CBHW040244100426
42811CB00011B/1149